Friendship Bracelets

Easy and Fun Eye-Catching Designs!

By Kaylee Conner

Mud Puddle inc.

NEW YORK

Friendship Bracelets
Easy and Fun Eye-Catching Designs!
by Kaylee Conner
Previously Printed as Beaded Friendship Bracelets

Copyright © 2008 by
Mud Puddle, Inc.
36 W. 25th Street
New York, NY 10010
info@mudpuddleinc.com

ISBN: 978-1-60311-149-2

Printed in China, May 2018

12 14 16 18 20 19 17 15 13 11

TABLE OF CONTENTS

INTRODUCTION

What exactly is a friend? Webster's dictionary defines friend "as someone who is not an enemy." To us, friends can be classmates, roommates, companions, confidantes, soul mates, allies, collaborators, teammates, peers, or supporters. A friend is a person that helps you, encourages you, questions you when she is in doubt, has fun with you, works with you, stands by you when you need her, and finally, needs you as much as you need her. A friend can be a casual friend, a good friend, a close friend, or your very best friend.

A friend is a person you want to do something nice for, whether it's a special occasion like their birthday, or just because it's Tuesday and you feel like it. A friend is a person that you want to thank in a "you're special to me" sort of handmade way.

That is why making friendship bracelets—for a friend or with a friend—is so much more meaningful than something store-bought. It's a special gift that you made with her in mind, something just for her. Remember, if it is made by hand, it comes from the heart.

Friendship bracelets are easy, fun, and inexpensive. You can make one or one hundred! Making unique bracelets for any occasion is simple—make them casual or dressy; beaded or plain; or from thread, ribbons, or strips of fabric. Your imagination is all you need to be a designer extraordinaire of friendship bracelets.

SUPPLIES

THREAD OR FLOSS:

Traditional six-strand embroidery thread, usually called embroidery floss, is most often used to make friendship bracelets.

SPECIALTY FIBERS:

Pearl cotton, knitting yarns, thin ribbons, soft silk-like fabrics, and specialty threads of any type can be used to make friendship bracelets.

TIPS

Make certain that the colors of the thread you are using will not bleed when wet. If you spend the time to make someone a friendship bracelet, you do not want it to get ruined.

Designer Secret:

The colors and textures of specialty fibers add a "designer touch" to even a simple project. Use them by themselves, or mix-and-match to make a variety of bracelets.

CLIPBOARD:

This book will refer to using a knotting board (see page 7), but you may prefer to use a clipboard rather than cardboard and pins to hold your bracelet while you are making it. This will secure the bracelet at the top, but you will be unable to pin the knots in place as you work.

KNOTTING BOARD:

We recommend creating a knotting board by using a thick piece of cardboard—such as the side of a box—to use as a work surface for creating your friendship bracelets. The board should be firm, yet allow you to easily insert and remove pins. Use large hatpins to secure your knots in place.

TIPS

By marking the end length of your bracelet on the knotting board or clipboard, you will know at a glance just how long the bracelet needs to be.

BEADS:

Beads of any type and size can be used to embellish your friendship bracelets. You will want to make certain that the thread or fiber you are using will fit through the hole of the bead. If you have difficulty getting the thread through the bead hole, you can use a beading wire loop (see page 8) to help you. If the bead hole is just too small, try adding a length of thin, 24-gauge wire to your threads. The beads will easily slip onto the wire.

BEADING WIRE LOOP:

This loop is optional, but can make it easier to add beads to your bracelet. Simply take a thin piece of 24-gauge wire, bend, and wrap as show in diagram.

EMBELLISHMENTS:

Almost anything can be used to adorn friendship bracelets. Charms for jewelry-making, small craft items such as miniature Christmas garlands, or a multitude of scrapbooking embellishments can be added. Walk up and down the aisles of your favorite fabric or craft store and see all of the wonderful things that can be used.

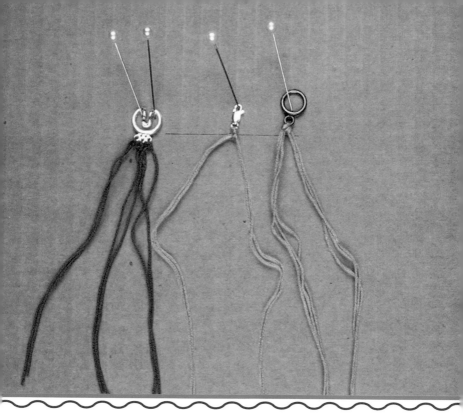

JEWELRY CLOSURES:

Jewelry closures are optional;
however, they make removing your
friendship bracelet a snap!
See Ending Your Bracelet
on page 14.

MISCELLANEOUS TOOLS AND MATERIALS:

24-Gauge Beading Wire
Fabric Glue
Ruler
Scissors

BASIC KNOTS

There are 3 basic knots used to make friendship bracelets in this book. They are easy to master and easy to remember, but you may want to practice a little before beginning to make your first friendship bracelet. A little practice now will save a considerable amount of frustration, time, and materials.

OVERHAND KNOTS

This knot can be created with as few as 2 threads, but you can use as many threads as you like.

Right Overhand Knot
Step 1
Measure at least 2 threads to be 4 times the length of the finished bracelet. (Double the length if you will be folding the threads in half before you start knotting.)

Tightly hold the left-hand thread and knot the remaining thread around it.

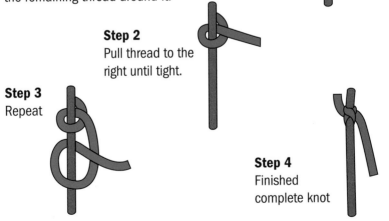

Step 2
Pull thread to the right until tight.

Step 3
Repeat

Step 4
Finished complete knot

Reminder: A complete overhand knot is always tied twice.

Left Overhand Knot
Step 1
Measure at least 2 threads to be 4 times the length of the finished bracelet. (Double the length if you will be folding the threads in half before you start knotting.)

Tightly hold the right-hand thread and knot the remaining thread around it.

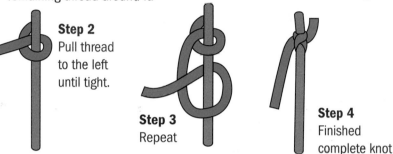

Step 2
Pull thread to the left until tight.

Step 3
Repeat

Step 4
Finished complete knot

Notes:

1. In this book the overhand knot is sometimes completed as a right overhand knot and sometimes as a left overhand knot, but either way it is the same knot.
2. The overhand knot can be made with as many threads as you want.

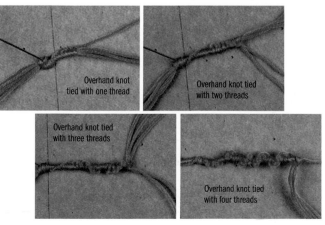

Overhand knot tied with one thread

Overhand knot tied with two threads

Overhand knot tied with three threads

Overhand knot tied with four threads

Reminder: *A complete overhand knot is always tied twice.*

SQUARE KNOT

Step 1
Measure each of 4 strands to be 4 times the desired length of the finished bracelet. Knot the strands together at one end, and pin the knot to the knotting board. Separate the strands.

Step 2
Move thread #4 from the far right and cross it over the center threads (#2 and #3) and under thread #1.

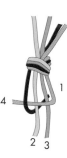

Step 3
Move thread #1 over thread #4 and under threads #2 and #3.

Step 4
Bring thread #1 from behind through the loop in thread #4 (far right).

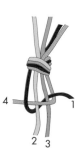

Step 5
Pull on threads #1 and #4 to create the first half of the square knot.

Step 6
Move thread #4 from the left and cross it over the center strands (#2 and #3) and under thread #1.

Step 7
Bring thread #1 under threads #2 and #3 and through the loop on the far left.

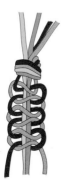

Step 8
Pull on threads #1 and #4 to finish the square knot.

ENDING YOUR BRACELET

Each of the projects in this book tells how to end the bracelet as it is pictured in the example. However, the following endings can be used with any of the bracelets you learn to make, so feel free to make any substitutions.

POSSIBILITY 1: LOOPED-END BRACELET

Folding the threads in half when starting the bracelet will create a loop at one end that can be used for tying bracelet ends together.

To Wear:
Wrap the finished bracelet around your wrist. Divide the threads at the loose end, and slip one half the threads through the loop. Tie to the other half of the threads, securing in a double knot so that the bracelet does not come untied.

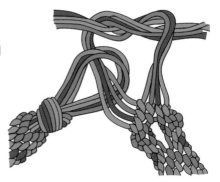

POSSIBILITY 2: LOOSE-ENDS BRACELET

This bracelet is made by using single strands of thread that are not folded in half and looped.

To Wear:

Wrap the finished bracelet around your wrist. Tie ends together in a double knot, cutting longer ends to desired length.

POSSIBILITY 3: JEWELRY CLOSURE BRACELET

These bracelets have jewelry closures at both ends just like traditional jewelry, making it possible to remove the bracelet as often as desired.

The closures are easiest to attach when the bracelet is made from 3 or 4 strands of embroidery floss. After tying the closures to the bracelet ends, you may need to place a small amount of fabric glue over the knots to keep them secure.

To Wear:

Attach this bracelet to your wrist just as you would attach any piece of traditional jewelry.

TIPS

Fastening your bracelets with Possibility 1 or Possibility 2 is best for those that will be worn until you tire of them. Tying and untying the threads will eventually fray them, making it difficult to tie a secure knot.

PROJECTS

The projects found in this book employ fun and easy techniques. Just follow the step-by-step instructions to create fabulous designs for you and your friends.

BASIC WRAPPED BRACELET

This easy bracelet requires a flexible core thread to wrap the threads of the bracelet around. Mix up the size of your bracelets by using a thin or thick core—and wear them singly or all together.

MATERIALS:

Core thread, thin
Embroidery floss, 1 color

STEP 1

Cut core thread to desired length of finished bracelet plus a little for finishing. Cut 2 strands of embroidery floss to 4 times the length of the core thread, tie both strands of floss to the core. Be sure to leave a long enough tail to tie your bracelet onto your wrist.

STEP 2

Pin the core thread to the knotting board. Tightly wrap both strands of floss around the core thread to the end and tie in a knot.

STEP 3

Wrap finished bracelet around wrist and tie floss ends together in a double knot. If ends are too long, trim to desired length.

WRAPPED BRACELET WITH ALTERNATING COLORS

Want to add a little variety to your wrapped bracelets? This simple bracelet alternates colors to let you and your friends show off your school colors, your club colors, or just your favorite colors.

MATERIALS:

Core thread, thin
Embroidery floss, 2 colors

STEP 1

Cut core thread to desired length of finished bracelet plus a little for finishing. Cut 2 strands of each color embroidery floss to 4 times the length of the core thread, tie all strands of floss to the core. Be sure to leave a long enough tail to tie your bracelet onto your wrist.

STEP 2

Pin the core thread to the knotting board. Tightly wrap the 2 strands of the first color of floss around the core and the second color of floss until you have the desired amount of color.

STEP 3

Pick up the strands of the second color floss and tightly wrap around both the core thread and the first color of floss until you have the desired amount of color.

STEP 4

Repeat Steps 2 and 3, alternating colors as desired until you reach the end of the core thread. Knot tightly at the end of the core thread.

STEP 5

Wrap finished bracelet around wrist and tie floss ends together in a double knot. If ends are too long, trim to desired length.

BASIC WRAPPED BRACELET WITH BEADS

MATERIALS:

Beads, 1 or more colors
Core thread, thin
Embroidery floss, 1 or more colors
Fabric glue (Optional)

These bracelets are made by following the steps for the Basic Wrapped Bracelet on page 16 or the Basic Wrapped Bracelet with Alternating Colors on page 18. After wrapping the core thread with the desired color(s) of floss, slip beads onto the bracelet. If beads need to be further secured into place, either secure with a dot of fabric glue or tie a piece of floss or thin ribbon on both sides of the bead or beaded section.

TWIST AND SHOUT!

MATERIALS:

Embroidery floss, 10 lengths—28" (63.5 cm) each

STEP 1

Tie all 10 floss strands in a knot, leaving a long enough tail to tie the bracelet to your wrist. Fasten the knot to the knotting board.

STEP 2

Hold the loose ends of the floss together and twist them several times until they are very tight.

STEP 3

Pull the twisted strands straight and place your finger in the center of the twisted length. Fold the twisted strands in half and remove your finger.

STEP 4

Remove the rope from your knotting board and knot the free ends together to create a double-knot effect. Trim uneven threads.

STEP 5

Wrap finished bracelet around your wrist. Divide the strands at the unlooped end of the bracelet, and slip half of the strands through the loop. Tie strand ends in a double knot so that your bracelet will not come untied.

Designer Secret:
String beads on one or more floss strands in step 1. Adjust beads as you wrap in step 2.

BRAIDED FRIENDSHIP BRACELETS

MATERIALS:

Assorted beads
Embroidery floss, 3 colors

STEP 1

Measure 3 colors of floss to 4 times the desired length of the finished bracelet and knot 1" (2.54 cm) from top of threads. Pin to the knotting board and braid desired length.

STEP 2

Thread beads onto floss and continue braiding to desired length.

STEP 3

Wrap finished bracelet around your wrist and tie floss ends together in a double knot. If ends are too long, trim to desired length.

BASIC WRAPPED BRACELET USING NOVELTY FIBERS

MATERIALS:

Core thread, thin
Novelty fiber(s)

These bracelets are made by following the steps for the Basic Wrapped Bracelet on page 16. Simply wrap the core thread with the novelty fiber(s) of your choice.

1-2-3 BRACELET

STEP 1

Cut a length of all 3 colors of floss 3 times the desired length of the finished bracelet. Tie all 3 lengths together and pin knot to knotting board, then separate threads as shown in diagram.

56" length

1 2 3

STEP 2

Weave the #3 thread over the #2 thread and under the # 1 thread, then over the #1 and under the #2 thread. Be careful to hold the threads straight and tight while you weave.

3

1 2

STEP 3

Hold the #1 and #2 threads with one hand and pull the #3 thread so that the weaving slides up the bracelet toward the top knot. Continue weaving for desired length.

3

1 2

STEP 4

Tie a knot at the end of the bracelet. Wrap finished bracelet around your wrist and tie thread ends together in a double knot. If ends are too long, trim to desired length.

MATERIALS:

Beads
Embroidery floss, 3 colors

Designer Secret:

For this bracelet create several woven strands plus 1 strand of beads strung on 24-gauge wire. At end of each strand secure a crimp bead and attach to jump ring and jewelry clasp. An easy alternative is to tie all strands and wire together in a knot at both ends of the bracelet and wrap around wrist.

Designer Secret:

Simply string typewriter beads over woven threads. Typewriter beads can be found in the scrapbooking section of your local craft store.

BASIC DIAGONAL STRIPE BRACELET

MATERIALS:

Embroidery floss, 4 colors

STEP 1

Measure and cut 1 strand of each color floss to 4 times the length of the finished bracelet. Tie a knot 2" (5 cm) from the top and pin to the knotting board.

STEP 2

Separate the threads.

STEP 3

Beginning with thread #1 on the far left, tie a complete overhand knot over thread #2.

STEP 4

Continuing with thread #1, make a complete overhand knot around each of the remaining threads.

Reminder: A complete overhand knot is always tied twice.

STEP 5

Thread #2 should now be on the far left. Begin the process again, tying complete overhand knots with thread #2 over threads #3, #4, and #1.

STEP 6

Continue knotting your threads in this manner until the bracelet is the desired length.

STEP 7

Tie a knot at the end of your bracelet. Trim the remaining thread to approximately 2" (5 cm).

STEP 8

Wrap finished bracelet around your wrist and tie the two knotted ends together.

TIPS

Hold each thread that is being tied straight and tight, pulling each knot you make to the same degree of snugness. This will give your finished bracelet a consistent texture.

BASIC DIAGONAL STRIPE BRACELET CONT.

Designer Secret:

Make a Diagonal Stripe Bracelet only make it twice as long as is usually needed. Add fiber crimps to the end threads along with a metal clasp. Twist the knotting so that it is tight and add charms attached to jump rings at regular intervals along the bracelet.

Designer Secret:

Make a Diagonal Stripe Bracelet using 3 colors of floss. Again make it twice as long, add fiber crimps, twist the knotting, and add oversized initial beads.

Designer Secret:

Make your Diagonal Stripe Bracelet only add an extra thread that is kept off to the side during the knotting of the threads. On this thread, string beads, wrap around the worked bracelet and tie the thread into the knot at the end.

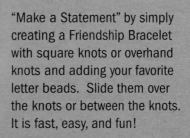

"Make a Statement" by simply creating a Friendship Bracelet with square knots or overhand knots and adding your favorite letter beads. Slide them over the knots or between the knots. It is fast, easy, and fun!

POM-POM FUN!

Using 4 strands of different colored embroidery floss do overhand knots switching the knotting thread at desired intervals.

With small colored safety pins that can be found in the scrapbook section of your local craft store pin different sized and colored pom-poms to the bracelet in the middle.

Make a bracelet using overhand knots and string letter beads to spell your and a friend's name on either side of 4 marble beads.

FELT FLOWERS

Remake the Diagonal Stripe Bracelet from Page 40 and glue felt flowers in the middle.